CONTENTS

Introduction

PART 1

THE IMPORTANCE OF LANGUAGE.

PART TWO
WRITING LETTERS

WRITING
BUSINESS AND PERSONAL
LETTERS, EMAILS AND TEXTS

Robert Fry

Straightforward Publishing
www.straightforwardco.co.uk

Straightforward Guides

British cataloguing in publication data. A catalogue record of this book is available from the British Library.

ISBN: 978-1-80236-006-6

Printed and bound by 4edge Ltd www.4edge.co.uk

Cover Design by BW Studio Derby.

Introduction

The relevance of the pandemic to writing business and personal letters

The onset of the pandemic, and the various lockdowns have led more and more people to work from home, through necessity. However, we still need to communicate in our daily lives for both work and personal matters – perhaps now more than ever.

The nature of business communication has, in particular changed due to COVID 19. There has been, without doubt an increase in email communication and communication by other media such as Zoom. Whether or not the art of writing personal letters has changed is another point. The main lessons still apply when creating successful and effective business and personal letters and emails and texts, as are illustrated throughout this book. The section covering business emails is particularly relevant.

The main point when producing letters, emails and text is that the writer must understand the very essence of the language in which he or she is writing. This involves understanding grammar and punctuation – in short understanding the basis of the language, in this case the English language.

Mastery of language and the ability to express oneself, in the business or personal domains, is a wonderful achievement. Mastery and effective use of language is akin to painting a beautiful picture.

This book dwells at the outset on grammar and punctuation and other finer points of the language. It shows the writer of the business or personal letter how to express what it is they are trying to say, how to lay it out and how to take care that the letter achieves its aim. The book is rigorous but rewarding. It does not seek to layout 50 different types of letter but to show the reader how to understand the complexities of the language and to coach the reader into a position where he or she will begin to enjoy the language more and to produce an effective letter, whether of a personal or business nature.

****

PART 1.

THE IMPORTANCE OF LANGUAGE

Chapter 1

The importance of Punctuation

There are a number of essential elements key to effective letter writing, whether business or personal letters. Basic punctuation is extremely important.

Consider how you speak to someone. Generally, what you say is not one long breathless statement. It is punctuated by full stops. When writing, think about how you would verbalise the same statement and insert full stops as appropriate. For example:

We went walking today and we stopped at a shop and bought something to eat and sat down and ate the food and then decided to move on we walked as far as we could before deciding to sit down and take a rest after half an hour we then decided to turn back------- Immediately, it is obvious that this statement is one long sentence which would leave the listener, or in turn the reader, confused. The correct version might be:

We went walking today, and we stopped at a shop and bought something to eat. We sat down and ate the food and then decided to walk on. We walked as far as we could before deciding to sit down and take a rest. After half an hour we decide to turn back.

The main point is that by inserting full stops we add structure to a sentence.

The use of commas

Whilst full stops are very important in order to add structure and also to separate out one sentence from the next, sometimes there can be a tendency to use commas instead of full stops. Commas have a particular role but can never take the place of full stops.

Commas are used to add a pause to a statement before concluding with a full stop. They are also used to separate items in a list. When using commas to separate items in a list the last one must be preceded by 'and'.

For example:

Dave liked swimming, football, ice hockey, mountain climbing, fell walking *and* judo.

Another example:

Peter was preparing his homework for the next day, his mother was cooking, his father was reading the paper and his sister was listening to music.

Beginning a sentence with a conjunction (joining word)

If you begin a sentence with a conjunction (joining word,) put a comma to separate the first part of the sentence from the rest of it. In this sentence, 'if' is a joining word and there is a comma after 'word'.

Here are two more examples with the conjunction underlined. Notice where the comma is placed:

Because it was snowing, we decided to stay inside.
As the sun set, the sky glowed.

Commas are used to separate groups of words within a sentence, in order to give statements within sentences more emphasis. Commas are used in many other areas too, such as before a question (I am not sure about that, are you?) or before a name (do be silent, Jack).

The most important element here, as with full stops, is that when you are composing a letter, think about what you are saying, to whom you are addressing it, and take time to punctuate the statement. This means that the person reading the letter can immediately relate to the contents and can interpret the message.

Making use of semi-colons, colons and the dash

The semi-colon is a very useful punctuation mark. It can be used when you feel that you do not need a full stop; usually the second statement follows closely to the first one. A capital letter is not used after a semi-colon. For example:

The road was getting busier; it was obvious that the traffic was starting to build up.

The idea of traffic building up follows on naturally from the road getting busier. In this case, it might be tempting to use a comma. However, as both statements follow on so closely a semi-colon is more appropriate.

The colon

A colon can be used for two purposes. It can introduce a list of statements, as in the following example:

There are two reasons why you failed: you lost your way, it was dark and you did not follow my orders.

Like the semi-colon you need no capital letter after the colon. The colon can also be used to show two statements reinforcing each other:

Your general punctuation is weak: you must learn to use the full stop and comma more effectively.

Using the dash

A dash is used for emphasis. What is said between dashes – or after the dash if there is only one – is more emphatic than if there were no dash. If you break your sentence in the middle to make an added point, use a dash before and after it:

Peter, Dave, Fred Grace – in fact everyone – had decided to go.

Use of the question mark

We have considered full stops, commas, semi-colons, colons and the use of the dash. We now need to consider the question mark. The question mark is obviously placed at the end of the question. You should always remember to include the question mark as, if it is missed, the reader of a letter might not take your question to be a question, but a statement.

Example

Is it raining outside?

You are not intending to go out in this weather, are you?

The second question is clearly a mixture of statement and question. To be understood as a question it is important to insert a question mark at the end. If you are using direct speech, the question mark takes the place of the comma and is always placed inside the inverted commas (speech marks):

'When are you going?' asked Susan.

Use of exclamation marks

The exclamation mark should be used rarely otherwise it loses its impact. It should not be used for emphasis; your choice of words should be sufficient to provide the necessary emphasis. It is used in direct speech, again in place of a comma. There should always be an exclamation mark if the word 'exclaimed' is used: 'I cannot believe you said that! She exclaimed.

Putting punctuation into practice.

Having discussed very basic punctuation, the main elements of which you will always use in letters, it is time to do a basic exercise.

Punctuate the following:

1. Dave was very angry with the garage he had bought the car from them and they had stated that the car was in perfect condition at least they had said that he would have no problem with it the car had been nothing but a problem and now he had lost his rag and decided to confront the owner and try to get his money or some of it back.

2. I don't think that is true she exclaimed

What don't you think is true he said?

It cannot be true that every time I go out I see the same person following me he seems to know my exact movements and I am very worried now.

3. I feel that I am knocking my head against a brick wall I have asked my mother father brother and sister what they think of my painting I felt that I had to ask them all by the way and all of them ignored me its as if I have offended them or something or they are to embarrassed to comment.

Now read the key points from Chapter 1.

****

Key points from Chapter 1

- Basic punctuation is one of the most important elements of effective letter writing.

- By inserting elements of punctuation we add structure to our letter.

- Whilst full stops are used to add structure, commas are used to add a pause and emphasis to a statement.

- Make effective use of colons, semi-colons and dashes.

- Question marks and exclamation marks must only be used when asking a question or adding emphasis.

Chapter 2

The Importance of Grammar

Making use of your sentence

Using nouns correctly

Nouns are a list of 'things'. The following are typical nouns: car, clock, computer, mechanic, spanners, and so on. Each of the above words can be the subject of a sentence if it is linked to a verb:

The garage *was* closed

The mechanic *arrived* late

The clock *fell* off the wall

The noun is the subject of the sentence and the verb, which is italicised in the above brief statements, is the doing word. A noun must be linked to a verb if it is to make sense.

Using verbs correctly

A verb is a 'doing' or 'being' word. There must be at least one verb in a sentence otherwise it is not a sentence.

Understanding verbs

Verbs can be either finite or non-finite.

Finite verbs

Finite verbs must show tense. They can be past, present or future and are always connected to a noun or pronoun. (more about pronouns later.)

Consider the verbs and tenses in the following statements:

Tomorrow I will travel to Bristol

Yesterday she was unhappy

He plays the guitar extremely well

'will travel' is the future tense.

'was' is the past tense.

'plays' is the present tense.

26

Non-finite verbs The non-finite verbs are the infinitive form of the verb and the present and past participles.

The infinitive

The infinitive is the form of verb that has 'to' before it:
To run, to sing, to eat, to walk.

Many people consider it incorrect to use a 'split infinitive'. This is when a word is placed between the 'to' and the verb:

It is difficult *to* accurately *assess* the data

The following example is better. The infinitive 'to assess' has not been 'split' by the adverb 'accurately'
It is difficult accurately *to* assess the data.

Past participles

The past participle is used with the verb 'to have'; it then forms a finite verb. Either the present or the past tense of the verb 'to have' can be used. It will depend on the context. Look at the following examples.

The past participles are italicised:

She had *scratched* her leg.

He has *passed* his driving test.

David has *prepared* supper.

Peter had *written* a letter to his father.

The first three participles in the examples above are the same as the ordinary past tense but 'has' or 'had' have been added. In the last example the past participle 'written' is different and can only be used with the verb 'to have'.

Present participle
The present participle always ends in '-ing' and is introduced by the verb 'to be'. The past or present tense of the verb 'to be' can be used:
David is *helping* his mother.

Susan was *washing* the car.

Using the gerund

The present principle can also be used as a noun. In this case it is called a gerund:

Shopping is fun.

The *wailing* was continuous.

Using the present participle as an adjective

Certain present participles can also be used as adjectives

The *crying* child ran to its mother.

The *howling* dog kept the family awake.

Now look at the following examples:

Rushed across the road.

Came into the shop.

Are these sentences? Of course they are not. Although they each have a verb, they have no subject linked to them. We don't know who rushed across the road or came into the shop. Add a noun and it makes sense:

The dog rushed across the road

The woman came into the shop.

In each sentence there must be a noun which is linked to a verb.

The above represents basic grammar, which, if linked with correct punctuation, helps you to structure a coherent and understandable letter that will be readily understood and will also instil a certain respect in the reader. If you require a more intense introduction to grammar there are a number of useful books on the market. Many colleges also run courses.

Paragraphing letters

Look at the following example:

John was very used to intimidating others. Every Saturday he would go into the local pub, sit there patiently until his friends started to drift in, and then begin hectoring them and generally 'winding them up'. Johns friends were very used to this and they put up with it because they knew him of old and, in many cases, gave as good as they got. One day, however, John sat as usual in the pub and he noticed that none of his friends had appeared, as was the norm. Another hour passed and still they had not showed up. John phoned Dave on his mobile. Dave answered and he stated that he was fed up with Johns hectoring, as were his friends. John wondered what to do in the face of the rejection of his friends. He was worried and it caused him to reflect on his behaviour. He came to the conclusion that he should visit them and discuss the problem.

The above is one long sentence, which should be broken into paragraphs. Paragraphs can vary into length but each paragraph deals with one topic. The positioning of the topic sentence can vary. The following example shows the above in paragraph form:

John was very used to intimidating others. Every Saturday he would go into the local pub, sit there patiently until his friends started to drift in, and then begin hectoring them and generally 'winding them up'. Johns friends were very used to this and they put up with it because they knew him of old and, in many cases, gave as good as they got.

One day, however, John sat as usual in the pub and he noticed that none of his friends had appeared, as was the norm. Another hour passed and still they had not showed up. John phoned Dave on his mobile. Dave answered and he stated that he was fed up with Johns hectoring, as were his friends. John wondered what to do in the face of the rejection of his friends. He was worried and it caused him to reflect on his behaviour. He came to the conclusion that he should visit them and discuss the problem.

Using quotation marks

Inverted commas are also used to enclose quotations and titles:

She went to the cinema to see the film 'Star wars'.

'A stitch in time saves nine' is a famous proverb.

The expression 'of the minds eye' comes from Shakespeare's play 'Hamlet'.

Notice that the full stop has been placed outside the inverted commas when the quotation or title is at the end of the sentence.

Now read the key points from Chapter 2, Grammar.

****

Key points from Chapter 2

- Nouns are a list of things, a verb is a doing word.

- There must be at least one verb in a sentence otherwise it is not a sentence.

- Verbs can be either finite or non-finite.

- The past participle is used with the verb 'to have'.

- The present participle always ends in '-ing' and is introduced by the verb 'to be'.

- By paragraphing letters you break down the flow of writing and introduce structure.

Chapter 3

Spelling

English spelling is not easy to learn. There are, of course, some rules. However, there are exceptions to these rules. Some spelling and pronunciation appear to be illogical. It is therefore very important that certain spellings are learnt.

There are 26 letters in the English alphabet. Five are vowels and the rest are consonants.

Forming words

The vowels are A,E,I,O,U. All words have to contain at least one vowel ('Y' is considered to be a vowel in words like 'rhythm' and 'psychology') Consonants are all the other letters that are not vowels. So that a word can be pronounced easily, vowels are placed between them. No more than three consonants can be placed together.

Overleaf are two lists.

The first contains some words with three consecutive consonants and the second are words with two consecutive consonants:

1. School, scream, chronic, Christian, through, splash.
2. Flap, grab, occasion, commander, baggage, added.

All the words in the examples have the consonants separated by vowels.

Forming plurals

To form a plural word an 's' is usually added to a noun. There are some exceptions. If a noun ends in 'y' and there is a consonant before it, a plural is formed by changing the 'y' into an 'i' and adding '-ies':

Lady = ladies
nappy = nappies
company = companies
berry = berries

If the 'y' is preceded by another vowel, an 's' only is added:

monkey = monkeys

donkey = donkeys

covey = coveys

If a noun ends in 'o' and a consonant precedes the 'o', '-es' is added to form a plural:

potato = potatoes

tomato = tomatoes

hero = heroes

If there is a vowel before the 'o' an 's' only is added:

studio = studios

zoo = zoos

patio = patios

Changing the form of a verb

When a verb ends in 'y' and it is necessary to change the tense by adding other letters, the 'y' is changed into an 'i' and 'es' or 'ed' is added:

He will *marry* her tomorrow

He was *married* yesterday

A dog likes to *bury* his bone

A dog always *buries* his bone

Using long vowels and short vowels

There is often a silent 'e' at the end of the word if the vowel is 'long':

Date, bite, hope, late, dupe.

Each of these words consists of one syllable (one unit of sound) if another is added, the 'e' is removed:

Date = dating

Bite = biting

And so on.

Adding '-ly' to adjectives

When forming an adverb from an adjective 'ly' (not ley) is added. If there is a 'y' at the end of the adjective, it must be changed to an 'i':

Adjective	*Adverb*
Happy	Happily
Beautiful	Beautifully

Quick	Quickly
Slow	Slowly

'I' before 'e' except after 'c'.

This rule seems to have been made to be broken. Some words keep to it but some break it. Here are some that follow the rule. All of them are pronounced 'ee' – as in 'seed':

No 'c' in front	*After 'c'*
niece	ceiling
piece	receive
grief	deceive

Exceptions to this rule are:

Neighbours, vein, either, neither, seize, weird.

Using a dictionary

Checking your spelling

Use a dictionary frequently to check your spelling. Don't guess the spelling of a word. Look it up. It is helpful to keep a list of words that you have misspelled so that you can learn them.

Looking at words

A dictionary not only tells you how to spell a word. It also tells you what part of speech the word is. Sometimes the word appears more than once as it has different meanings and can be used as a different part of speech.

Look at the following examples:

Land (noun) (a) The solid part of the earth

             (b) A country

Land (verb)

             (c) To go ashore or bring a plane down to the
ground

The dictionary will also often give the derivation of a word. English is a rich language that owes much to other languages. If you have time, browse through a dictionary looking at the derivation of some of the words. It can be a fascinating experience.

Making use of the thesaurus

A thesaurus can be very useful. It will help you to find an alternative word (synonym) for a word that you have used too much. Words are shown alphabetically and beside each will be a list of words that could replace the word that you want to lose. Not all synonyms will be suitable. It depends on the context of the word.

Now read the key points from Chapter 3, spelling, overleaf.

****

Key points from Chapter 3

- There are 26 letters in the English alphabet, 5 are vowels and the rest consonants.

- Every word has a vowel

- No more than three consonants can be placed together.

- Use a dictionary frequently to check your spelling.

- A thesaurus will provide many alternatives to a word.

Chapter 4

Apostrophes and Abbreviations

Using apostrophes to show possession

Apostrophes are put at the end of nouns when the nouns have something belonging to them.

Making a singular noun possessive

If a noun is singular and it has something belonging to it, add an apostrophe and an 's'. For singular words that show possession the apostrophe is always placed before the 's':

Karen's handbag was stolen.

Her neighbour's fence was blown down.

The child's ball bounced over the wall.

If the singular noun already ends in an 's' another 's' should still be added:

The princess's bridal gown was made by a well-known couturier.

The thief stole the Duchess's jewels.

However, in some cases, the extra 's' can be omitted as in the following cases:

James' book was missing

He damaged his Achilles' tendon.

Making a plural noun possessive

Most nouns add an 's' to make a plural. In this case the apostrophe goes after the noun if it is possessive:

The thundering of the horses' hoofs broke the silence.

The ladies' gowns were beautiful.

Some nouns do not add an 's' to become a plural. In this case, if they are possessive, they are treated like singular nouns. The apostrophe is added before the extra 's'. Some of these words are: children, men, women, mice, sheep, geese:

The children's playground was vandalised.

Kate watched the mice's tails disappearing round the corner.

Using possessive pronouns correctly

When using the possessive form of a pronoun, apostrophes are not used. The possessive pronouns are: mine, her, his, its, ours, yours and theirs.

The blame is mine (no apostrophe)

These books are hers (no apostrophe)

The first prize was his (no apostrophe)

Abbreviating words

When writing formally, it is better not to abbreviate. Write the words out in full. However, it is, of course, acceptable to abbreviate when writing dialogue.

*

Using apostrophes to abbreviate words

An abbreviation is when letters are missed out. Sometimes two words are combined into one. An apostrophe is placed where the letter or letters have been omitted:

'Do not' = don't

'Can not' = can't

'Would not' = wouldn't

Note especially that 'Could have' becomes 'could've' not 'could of'. Because of the way the abbreviation in the above example sounds, a common mistake is to use the word 'of' instead of the abbreviation 've'.

Abbreviating words without using apostrophes

When words are shortened, it is usual to put a full stop at the end:

information info.

document   doc.

etcetera   etc.

The names of counties are shortened in the same way and all have full stops after them:

Berkshire Berks.

Nottinghamshire Notts.

Other words that are often abbreviated are titles but some of these should only be abbreviated if the title is followed by the person's full name. A full stop should be put after the abbreviation if it is used:

Capt. Edward Symes

not

Capt. Symes

Handling contractions

Some words are abbreviated by using the first and last letters only. These are contractions of the original word and do not usually need a full stop at the end:

Mister   Mr

Mistress Mrs

Doctor   Dr

No full stop is needed after a contraction.

Using acronyms

It is becoming increasingly common to describe companies or organisations only by the initial letters of the names of the group. This is called an acronym. This is now so prevalent that we often forget what the original letters stood for. It is no longer considered necessary to put a full stop after each capital letter. Here are some reminders of frequently used acronyms:

RADA   Royal Academy of Dramatic Arts

NATO   North Atlantic Treaty Organisation

ASH   Action on Smoking and Health

UNICEF United Nations Children's Fund

RAF   Royal Air Force

And many more!

Now read the key points from Chapter 4, apostrophes and abbreviations.

****

Key points from Chapter 4

- Apostrophes are put at the end of nouns when the nouns have something belonging to them.

- If a noun is singular and it has something belonging to it, add an apostrophe and an 's'. For singular words that show possession the apostrophe is always placed before the 's.

- Most nouns add an 's' to make a plural. In this case the apostrophe goes after the 's' if it is possessive.

- When writing formally, it is better not to abbreviate.

- It is becoming more popular to use acronyms to abbreviate companies or organisations.

Chapter 5

Using the Correct English

Recognising common mistakes

Remember that punctuation is essential if your work is to make sense.

- Do not use commas instead of full stops. If in doubt, put a full stop.
- Remember to put a question mark at the end of a question.

Revising sentence construction

Remember that sentences must make sense. Each sentence must contain at least one subject (noun) and one verb. If there is more than one verb, there are two clauses and these should either be separated by a full stop or a semi-colon or linked by a conjunction.

Revising the correct use of verbs

Always make sure that the nouns and verbs 'agree'. If the noun is singular, the verb should always be singular.

Remember that collective nouns are singular and are followed by the singular form of the verb.

The politician is hoping to win tonight.

not

The politician *are* hoping to win tonight.

Avoiding the misuse of pronouns

There is often confusion in the words 'I' and 'me', 'she' and 'her', 'he' and 'him', 'we' and 'us', 'they' and 'them'.

'I', 'she', 'he', 'we', and 'they', are personal pronouns and are usually the subject of the sentence. This means they are the instigators of the action in the sentence:

I like travelling

*S*he went on holiday

*H*e went home

We have no bread

They are going today

'Me, 'her', 'him', 'us', and 'them', are usually the objects of the sentence. This means that something is done to them:

The stone hit *me*

The prize was given to *her*

The wall collapsed on *him*

The dog bit *us*

The mother scolded *them*

Revising spelling

Learn the most commonly misspelled words; for example:

Surprise, disappear, disappoint, independent

Learn the correct spelling of words that sound the same but are spelt differently; for example:

hear - here

their - there

sea - see

too - two - to

The words 'practice' and 'practise' are often confused and so are 'advice' and 'advise'. 'Practise' and 'advise' are the verbs and 'practice' and 'advice' are the nouns:

You must practise the guitar if you are to improve.

There is a cricket practice at the net today.

I advise you not to do that

Please take my advice.

Other words that are often confused are 'council' and 'counsel', 'compliment' and 'compliment', 'principle' and 'principal' and 'stationery' and 'stationary'.

Avoiding common mistakes

A mistake that is often heard is the following:

He is very different *to* his brother.
This is not correct and should read:
He is very different *from* his brother.

If you **differ,** you move away from. If you are **similar** you are similar to.

Avoiding mistakes when using apostrophes and abbreviations

- Do not put an apostrophe every time there is a plural word ending in 's'.
- The abbreviation of 'could have' is 'could've' not 'could of'.
- Do not put a full stop after a contraction:

Doctor - Dr

Mister - Mr

Avoiding unnecessary repetition

- Remember that nouns do not usually need to be repeated within the same sentence.
- Replace them with pronouns

He tried on his new boots. The boots were too tight.

This should be:

He tried on his new boots. *They* were too tight.

Avoiding tautologies

A tautology is where the same thing is said twice over in different ways, for example:

The last chapter will be at the end of the book.

The people applauded by clapping their hands.

These two sentences are repetitious. The meaning is at the beginning of the sentence and has been repeated again at the end. Avoid tautologies.

Varying the sentence

If sentences frequently begin with the same word, the word becomes monotonous. Avoid the temptation to start consecutive sentences in the same way.

She went to the car. She opened the trunk. She closed the trunk. She was upset.

These sentences all start with she so the passage does not flow. It is easy to say the same thing in another way so that it does flow:

Susan went to the car and opened the trunk. Closing the trunk, she was clearly upset.

Making comparisons

When using adjectives to compare two things or people '-er' is usually added to the base word:

big   bigger

tall   taller

slow   slower

happy   happier

When more than two people are involved, '-est' is added to the adjective:

Big   bigger   biggest

Tall   taller   tallest

Slow   slower   slowest

Some words are so constructed that to add the suffix '-er' or '-est' would produce clumsy words. In this case 'more' and 'most' are put before the adjective instead:

beautiful   more beautiful   most beautiful

intelligent more intelligent   most intelligent

Eliminating jargon

The word 'jargon' derives from a Middle English word meaning 'meaningless chatter'. The derivation suggests a very good reason why jargon should be avoided. Anyone who is a member of a group uses jargon that is intelligible only to other members of the same group.

Lawyers have their own jargon and so do politicians, schoolteachers and nurses. You should use words and expressions that can be easily understood by all and not forms of language that have grown up around professions, for example, as these can often serve to confuse unless you are part of that group.

An example of such words can be words that end in 'ise'. Privatise, normalise, prioritise and so on. Make sure that you use language which is not restricted and is in common use.

Avoiding clichés

Clichés are phrases that are heard over and over again. We all use them and they are often very apt.

Creating similes

'White as a sheet' and 'ran like the wind' are similes. These are comparisons between two things using the words 'like' or 'as'. Many clichés are similes and they are often very vivid. However, they are not original and you should avoid them.

Using metaphors

Metaphors are also comparisons but they are 'implied' and do not use 'like' or 'as'. We use metaphorical language a great deal in everyday speech. It is language that is not literally true but cannot be classified as a lie as everyone knows what is meant.

Look at the following examples:

I'm starving.

He says he's freezing

She's dying of thirst.

All are clichés and all are metaphors. The language is metaphorical – not literally true. If it were true, all three characters would be dead and we know that is not what is meant.

Improving your style

Economising on words

Good writing is simple and easy to understand. Unnecessary words should be eliminated. If one word can replace four then use it.

Using the active voice

The active voice is more positive than the passive voice. In the active voice a subject does something. In the passive voice something is done to him.

Active voice

The father struck his son

The teacher gave his class a detention

Passive voice

The son was struck by his father

The class was given a detention by the teacher

Avoiding negatives

Using positive statements instead of negative ones also economises on words.

For example:

He did not remember his wife's birthday.

Clare was not present in the afternoon.

Would be better as the following:

He forgot his wife's birthday

Clare was absent in the afternoon.

Avoid double negatives which make a positive:

There isn't no one there

I haven't got no lunch

The word 'not' and 'no' cancel each other out and therefore the first example means that there is someone there and the second means that I have got lunch.

There is a choice of two correct versions. Only one negative should be used if the sense is to be kept:

There isn't anyone there.

Or

There is no one there.

I haven't got any lunch.

or

I have no lunch.

Developing your own style

By now you should have a good grasp of the basics of English and you should aim to develop your own style of writing. Avoid repetition and vary your sentences. Look at a cross section of other people's styles and begin to develop a style of your own. The art of writing is a very satisfying art, particularly when done with care and attention.

Now read the key points from Chapter 5 overleaf.

****

Key points from Chapter 5.

- Do not use commas instead of full stops. If in doubt put a full stop.

- Each sentence must contain at least one noun and one verb.

- Avoid the misuse of pronouns.

- Learn the most commonly misspelled words.

- Avoid common mistakes.

- Avoid unnecessary repetition.

- Avoid tautologies.

- Try to vary sentences.

- Eliminate jargon and avoid clichés.

- Economise on words and develop your own style.

PART 2

WRITING LETTERS

Chapter 6

Writing Business letters

Having studied the basics of English grammar, it is now time to construct an effective letter.

Aiming your letter

Letters project images of you and your organisation to the broad outside world. Clients and general customers of your business will build up a picture of you and your organisation from the style of letter that you write.

When you write a letter you should consider to whom you are addressing it. What is the aim of your letter? A clear aim will tell the reader what he or she wishes to know, but also helps you as a writer by telling you what you do not need to write.

A letter provides a permanent record of transactions between organisations. That record will guide future actions and may also appear as evidence in cases where contractual problems are arising and court action is necessary. Your record must be clear and correct.

Ask why you are writing and then you can focus on what your letter is aiming to achieve:

- payment of an overdue account
- sales of a new product
- technical information
- confirmation of a meeting

Who is your reader?

You should give thought to the person who will read your letter. For incoming letters seek guidance from:

- the name of the job or department title at the end
- the content of the letter

If you are initiating correspondence, make sure that you have targeted your reader accurately. It might be worth making a telephone call to ask who deals with a certain area. Once you have done this you can direct your request to the most appropriate person. Buyer and salesman have a different outlook on a similar product. In making a technical enquiry to the buyer you will expect a competent reply: the salesman's competence may direct you to the benefit of buying the product.

One very important point is that the level of your writing must be your natural way of expressing your meaning. If you try to adopt any other style than the one that is natural to you, you will emerge as strained and unnatural.

What does your reader need?

When you respond to a letter, take a close look at what it requires:

- Is it looking for information?
- Does it need action?
- What action does it require and by when?

Consider how to approach the task

Writing acts as a window through which the reader may see the personality that lies behind the words. In certain cases, this can be a disadvantage, for example if you have an indifferent attitude or if other factors have influenced your mood. This will be reflected in the letter. You have to remember that when people read letters they will pick up varied messages, depending on their own personality and your mood and style when writing the letter.

There are advantages. Once that you are aware that your attitude shows in your writing then you can use this to considerable effect. Do not try to hide your personality, let the reader see that you are able to understand the readers problems, that you are willing to help or that you are patient if a mistake has been made or incomplete information has been given.

Your approach will obviously vary considerably depending on who you are writing to. If you are writing to complain about poor service you will expect to be firm in your tone. You are likely to be plain speaking, specifying what is wrong and laying out timescales for action.

If you are writing in reply to a complaint from a customer, a firm approach will be inappropriate. You will need to adopt a different, more conciliatory approach.

In professional firms, letters rarely go beyond the conventional picture of three short paragraphs. These letters may be:

- offering advice of some sort, such as financial advice
- specifying an architects detailed requirements for progress on a job

In handling more extended material you will need a more complete and visible classification of the content. This will show in headings, and perhaps sub-headings within the narrative, to give the required direction to the reader.

Decide where and when to write

The place and timing of your letter is critical. The reader will not be very happy if your letter arrives on the morning that a crucial decision has to be made, a decision which will be influenced by your letter. Neither will that person be happy if the letter goes to the wrong address. This can easily happen where businesses are organised around different addresses. Your sales letter must arrive at the time that relates to the budget, or the buying decision. At the same time it must be persuasive enough to encourage the reader to put it on record in anticipation of such a time.

Now read the key points from Chapter Six, Writing Business Letters.

Key points from Chapter Six

- Letters project images of you and the organisation to the outside world.

- When you write a letter, you should consider to whom you are addressing it.

- A letter provides a permanent record of transactions between organisations.

- Decide when and where to write a letter.

****

Chapter 7

Planning and Structuring a Letter

Many people who write letters do so in a hurry and will not give a great amount of time or thought to the contents. In some cases, this may be suitable, especially if you are writing a very short letter of acknowledgement. However, in longer business letters that require more elaboration, then this is not appropriate and a great deal more thought needs to be exercised.

A relatively small amount of time is needed to plan and write letters and, in the long run, will save you time and effort. A well-planned letter will ensure that you communicate the right amount of information and detail to the reader.

Many writers sometimes have problems with the opening sentence of a letter. There is the idea that the opening sentence is of the utmost importance and that the rest will flow easily. This is not always the case. When planning a letter, work from the general to the particular. The detail will then tend to fall naturally into place.

The contents of your letter

When determining the content of your letter, you should ask yourself:

- who is my reader?
- What does that person need to know?

If that person needs to know very little, for example that you intend to be at a meeting, a few words will suffice. However, if the person wishes to know quite a lot then you will need to be very methodical in planning the contents of the letter. When approaching such a task:

- gather relevant information
- allocate the information to main sections
- give each main section a heading

With classification it is tempting to choose general or abstract headings that allow the detail to fit comfortably. You will achieve a better result by choosing more selective, more concrete headings.

Decide the sequence of delivery

It is difficult to think about the content of your letter without giving thought to the sequence in which you will deliver it. A natural order will quite often emerge. When you are resolving a problem:

- what has gone wrong
- why it went wrong
- what will we do to put it right

When you review activity:

- what we have done in the past
- how we operate currently
- what we plan for the future

A natural order promotes a logical flow of thinking and allows the letter to end at the point you wish to reach:

- looking ahead rather than looking back
- solving a problem rather than raising one

For more complicated letters people tend to group their material functionally but find the sequence more challenging and often repeat material. To plan your sequence:

- spread your headings across the top of a sheet of A4 using the landscape or horizontal plane.
- List the points that relate to each heading in columns
- Consider any changes in the sequence
- Decide whether larger sections should break down into sub-headings or whether additional headings would be better.

An outline classification can show your intended approach to a colleague or other. Changes are easy to make and the outline classification will serve as an excellent prompt for your draft letter.

Forming paragraph structure

We discussed paragraph structures earlier on. There are no rules for paragraphing that require text to be broken after a certain number of words or line. Paragraphs have a lot more to do with consistency of thought than length. However, there are guidelines that help to convert planned content into readable paragraphs:

- change paragraph with each change of subject

- if your subject requires lengthy exploration, break it into further paragraphs that reflect the different aspects.
- Headline your paragraph to give an early indication of your subject.

Many business letters are brief and to the point and can be delivered in a single paragraph. The key is to ensure that the reader can follow your train of thought and that your letter is not one long rambling monologue.

Many single page business letters appear in a three-paragraph format that reflects:

- identification
- explanation
- action

In these cases the opening and closing paragraphs are often short – commonly a single sentence. The middle paragraph expands to the extent that it is necessary to complete.

Paragraph length is also about a particular writing style. A single sentence can make an emphatic paragraph but over-use of single sentence paragraphs will diminish their effect.

Control your sentence length

Writers struggling to construct a sentence are usually concerned with finding the right words to convey their intended meaning to the reader. You should avoid the long lead-in to a sentence. Your lead-in should be snappy and direct as opposed to long winded. If you find it difficult to express your thoughts you should think to yourself, what exactly am I trying to say?

Researchers have measured writing to see what makes it readable. Answers usually include the types of words used and the sentence length. The ideal sentence length is usually about twenty words. After this a sentence can tend to become unwieldy.

Words are not just counted between full stops: the colon and semi-colon also determine the sentence structure for this purpose.

You should remember that you are seeking a readable average sentence length: you are not trying to make every sentence twenty words long. Variety in sentence length will produce a more interesting style. You should adopt a conversational approach in your writing, controlling your sentence length.

Use a range of punctuation

Again, in chapter 2, we looked at punctuation generally. Relating this directly to letter writing, the trend is to use only the punctuation you need to reveal your meaning.

The full stop

A sentence must contain a subject and a finite verb; a finite verb is a verb that has been modified by its subject. A sentence must express a complete thought but can have a very simple structure:

David writes

It is snowing

Semicolon

The semicolon provides a useful pause, lighter than the full stop but heavier than a comma. You will use it most reliably by ensuring that the elements you have linked could appear as independent sentences.

Colon

Many writers in business use the colon to introduce a list:

During the recent visit to the exhibition, the following items were lost: one briefcase, one wallet, one umbrella and a set of keys. The colon also allows you to define or illustrate an initial statement:

Following my operation, my personal circumstances changed somewhat: I found myself short of money and unable to work.

Commas

There are many technical reasons for using commas but these are mainly to do with building a pause to indicate your meaning on first reading.

- use a comma when you wish to indicate such a pause
- do not break a sentence, unnecessarily with a comma
- Do not use a comma if you need a heavier stop, this section applies even if the next point is linked. (a semi-colon should replace the comma here).

Brackets

Brackets enclose an aside or illustration and need no further punctuation.

There are 5280 feet (or 1760 yards) in a mile

It is useful for husband and wife (in certain circumstances) to hold a joint bank account.

Question marks

Use question marks only for direct questions.

Where are you going?

When are you going to send the cheque?

Now read the key points from Chapter Seven overleaf

****

Key points from Chapter Seven

- Business letters cannot, usually, be written in a hurry. This is especially the case if they are longer letters trying to convey complex information.

- When planning a letter, work from the general to the particular.

- When determining the contents of a letter, you should ask who is your reader and what do they need to know.

- Decide the sequence of delivery.

- Structure your letter.

- Control your sentence length.

- Use a range of punctuation.

Chapter 8

Layout of Letters

Letters always have a certain convention that distinguishes them from e-mail and memorandum. Letters always begin 'Dear............' and end 'Yours sincerely.........'. This is the same whatever the nature and tone of the letter, whether you are writing a strong letter of complaint or a more measured letter.

However, letters have become less formal and word processing now gives many more options for the alignment and appearance of text than a layout that was once dictated by the limitations of a typewriter.

The majority of letters are left aligned only, leaving a ragged right margin that appears less formal and aids reading. Key information such as the reference, date, address, salutation, complimentary close and enclosures is increasingly aligned to the left margin.

Letterheads have changed too. Once all information appeared at the top of the page. Now you may see the company logo prominent at the top but much of the statutory detail at the foot.

Quote references in full

We put a reference on a letter so that when someone replies quoting the reference, we are easily able to find the letter on file. Always quote a reference when replying. Much correspondence is stored electronically and the quoted reference may be the only manageable way of retrieving a particular letter.

One common layout will begin:

Reference

Date

Address of reader

. . . .

. . . .

An alternative layout will show:

Address of reader   Your ref:

            Our ref:

………………...   Date:

………………...

………………...

In the second example, the information will often appear in print on the company letterhead and the position will reflect the letter template on the word processor.

You should look at the address not simply to direct your letter to the receiving organisation but to the individual from whom you seek a response. It is now usual practice to include the name and job title of the recipient as part of the address. As that information appears through the window of the envelope your information can be targeted unopened to the reader.

Choose an appropriate salutation

Try to include the name in the salutation at the start of your letter. This will:

- get commitment from a reader whom you have targeted precisely
- set a personal tone for your writing

Writers sometimes identify themselves with just name and initials at the end of a letter. However, there is a practical problem in that we need to attach a style (Mr Mrs Miss Ms) to the reply. Very formal style still appears in business letters. You may find a letter that begins:

For the attention of Mrs D Smith

Dear Sirs
We acknowledge receipt of your recent letter...............

A name allows you to be more natural and direct:

Dear Mrs Smith

Thank you for...........

You will need a formal salutation when you write to an institution rather than a named reader.

A PLC or a limited company is a single legal entity and it is logical to address the company as Dear Sir. Avoid writing Dear Sir/Madam. Whichever part of that generalisation applies to it, it is offensive for its failure to relate properly to you. A general name can make a good alternative.

Use informative headings

Most letters will benefit from a heading. This serves to:

- tell the reader what you are writing about
- provides a descriptive reminder of the content of a letter you may later wish to retrieve.

In an extensive letter distinguish between a heading that covers the broad scope of the letter at the start:

Pullfir Contracts

Annual check J.Peters

Training programme

And the more specific headings that occur at intervals to identify the specific topics of the letter.

In a short letter you may write predominantly on one topic but then wish to make a small unrelated point later. This need produces clichés like:

May I take this opportunity to remind…………..

While you are right to take the opportunity you will make a clear case by putting your thought under a separate heading. The letter will take on the following form:

Salutation

Heading one

. . . .

. . . .

. . . .

Heading Two

. . . .

Close

Think about the sequence in which you handle your headings. Where possible end with the topic that needs action. Bullet points form a practical sub-structure for letters. They are best for items that require separate identification but which need no specific reference.

Before we can authorise a mortgage we will require:

- three payslips
- your P60
- proof of residence.

A sub-structure of numbers is helpful where you wish to raise a number of points which require a specific answer from your reader.

Start with the reasons for writing

Use the start of your letter to identify the reason for writing in the first place. When you initiate correspondence, spell out your intention for the reader. A heading will provide the initial view but your opening sequence will sharpen the focus:

- I am writing for information about the catering facilities that you offer.
- I plan to visit Sweden in the Summer

When responding to a letter you have a similar need to provide a clear focus for the reader. You may wish to use the heading from the original letter before responding more specifically:

- Thank you for your letter of 12th July.
- I confirm that our latest range of books will be ideal for your school.

- The plan enclosed with this letter should enable us to progress the matter.

Some very short letters end where they begin:

- Please send me a copy of your latest book and a catalogue
- I can confirm that I will be at the finance meeting next week

End by pointing the way ahead

The end of your letter is important in triggering the action you seek from the reader:

- Please let me know when you will send me my cheque.
- Please send me the completed form with payment by July 16th.

The true aim of the letter may vary from the issue that has prompted it. In such cases project your purpose at the end.

Long letters containing a number of action points may benefit from a short summary of actions at the end. Avoid clichés at the end of your letter. These usually appear when you have covered the ground and are ready to sign off.

Padding at this point pushes the required action further back into the letter, making it less of a prompt for the reader's attention.

Matching the end of the letter to the salutation

There is a firm convention for matching the ending of a letter to the opening. If you begin with a proper noun:

Dear Mr Smith

Dear Miss Jones

You end:

Yours sincerely (the 's' is always lower case)

Similarly if you begin with a common noun:

Dear Leaseholder

Dear Lord Mayor

You end:

Yours sincerely

For formal salutations:

Dear Sir

Dear Madam

You end:

Yours faithfully

Composing Business letters

Writing effective letters is not just detailing information. The way you compose the letter, the format, is very important indeed. As well as the reader of the letter, you will need to consider:

- the sequence in which you deliver your letter
- the tone reflected in your choice of language.

Ask yourself, when putting the letter together:

- how firm should you be?
- should you be apologetic?
- Should you send enclosures?

And so on.

The sequence of a letter allows you to move:

- from where you are now
- by means of any supporting information
- to where you want to be.

Choosing an appropriate tone

When you write, your language conveys the content of the letter and the manner of its delivery. You should think very carefully about the words you use and the way you use them. Obviously, each letter is different and, in the context of business, there are many situations that you will need to address, from taking action against a member of staff, against a supplier, to praising someone for good work to chasing late payments.

One strand linking all letters is that of getting to the point as quickly as possible whilst getting the message across. The use of language is an art and a skill and it is very necessary to ensure that you have said all that you have to say, in a clear and (often) sensitive fashion. The aim is to get your message across and to convince or persuade the other of your case.

Summary and sample business letters.

In the last three chapters, several key points have been stressed. Before laying out sample business letters it is important to summarise these points:

- Aim your letter carefully. You should ask yourself why you are writing and who is your intended recipient. What does your reader need?
- Make sure you plan and structure your letter and decide the sequence of delivery. Take pains to ensure that your punctuation is correct and also control your sentence length.

Sample business letters

Overleaf.

Introducing your firm

PRINTING SERVICES LIMITED

Mr D Davies	42 Smiths Drive
Askews Castle Ltd	Aberdeen
38 King Road	Perthshire
London	Scotland
E17 4PT	

Tel: 020 8123 5467

Our ref: 321

21st July 20

Dear Mr Davies,

I am writing to introduce my company to you. We care a business that provides printing services, consultancy and printing machinery to companies in the north of England. Our clients include Nobles, Bloomsbury and Polestar Wheaton Limited. In particular we offer:

- Cost effective printing solutions to meet all requirements.
- Consultancy services. These are designed to ascertain a clients needs.
- Follow up work with recommendations and costing.

At this stage, we enclose our latest brochure for your perusal. If you are interested in our products and services either now or in the future, please call me on my direct line 020 8123 5467. We would be pleased to supply further details on request or to discuss your requirements further.

Yours sincerely

David Askew

Sales manager

**

Offering new products

PRINTING SERVICES LIMITED

Mr D Davies   42 Smiths Drive

Askews Castle Ltd   Aberdeen

38 King Road   Perthshire

London   Scotland

E17 4PT

Tel: 020 8123 5467

Our ref: 321

21st July 20

Dear Mr Davies,

We are pleased to introduce the latest addition to our fast expanding range of printing presses, the Digital plus reproduction unit. This innovative product is the latest in a line of presses introduced by Printing Services Limited. It is designed to enable small publishers to cut costs and keep their stock holdings down. There are two distinctive features that distinguishes our press from others:

- Low print runs of 1 or more can be achieved.
- The press can achieve a two-week turnaround from placing of the order to fulfilment.

For a limited period, we are making a special offer available exclusively to our customers: This is a 10% discount off the normal trade price for each press ordered.

We enclose sales literature for the press. To take advantage of this offer please ring me direct on 020 8123 5467. Please note that this offer is for a limited period. We look forward to receiving your call.

Yours sincerely

David Askew
Sales Manager

**

Chasing a reluctant buyer

PRINTING SERVICES LIMITED

Mr D Davies   42 Smiths Drive

Askews Castle Ltd   Aberdeen

38 King Road   Perthshire

London   Scotland

E17 4PT

Tel: 020 8123 5467

Our ref: 321

24th July 20

Dear Mr Davies,

We were delighted to receive your enquiry about our printing press last week. I understand that you expressed interest following a demonstration by our agent. We were sure that you would be impressed with the press and would appreciate the advantages to your company.

We can confirm that this product is still available at a 10% discount to you. However, we have to point out once again that this offer can extend for a limited period only as we have received many expressions of interests and resultant firm sales.

I am pleased to enclose our sales literature for your further perusal and information. Please do not hesitate to contact me to discuss the purchase of our press.

We look forward to hearing from you again.

Yours sincerely

David Askew
Sales manager

The three letters above demonstrate all of the key aims of a business letter. The letter is aimed at the key person, the message is clear. There is a clear understanding of what the reader needs. The letter is planned, structured and the sequence of delivery leaves the reader in no doubt as to the message.

The sentences are short, crisp and to the point. The reader will be very clear about the intent and will be impressed by the layout.

There are many varieties of business letters but the key themes are exactly the same throughout.

Now read the key points from Chapter 8

****

Key points from Chapter 8

- Letters have a certain convention that distinguishes them from e-mail and memoranda.

- Quote any references in full.

- Choose an appropriate salutation.

- Use informative headings.

- Start with the reasons for writing.

- End by pointing the way ahead.

- Choose an appropriate tone.

Chapter 9

Writing Personal letters

So far, we have concentrated on the nature and form of business letters. These letters, by their nature, require a great deal of attention to detail as they act primarily as records of business and need to be specific in their aim.

Personal letters, whilst also ideally needing the same level of knowledge of the English language and attention to detail, have a different starting point. This is that they are personal and are often written to people we know and have conversed with many times. Therefore, many elements that we need to be aware of in business letters, such as the avoidance of jargon and clichés, are quite often present in personal letters.

Nevertheless, there are certain formal conventions that need to be observed at the outset.

Personal salutations

The personal letter will differ from the business letter in that you will usually put your name and address on the top right hand side, as with the example overleaf and the date under the address.

The letter will, in many cases, be handwritten, to add to the feeling of intimacy, and will finish not with 'Yours sincerely' but quite often will finish with 'love, or 'regards' or even 'cheers', depending on who you are writing to and how you have written the letter.

See example letter overleaf

Example personal letter.

38 Cromwell Road

Walthamstow

London E17 9JN

3rd May 20

Dear Peter,

It was really great to see you at the opening match of the world cup last Wednesday. Hey, what a great game wasn't it? I really loved the first half and, although the second half dragged a bit there was loads of action.

Did you see Stanley Peters? What a real snake in the grass! He was excellent in the first half but was real lazy in the second. He should have been substituted.

Anyway, enough about football. What about you and your family? I hope that you are all faring well and Susan is OK. She is a really nice person and you have a very good partner there.

Well, old buddy, enough said. Once again, it was really great to see you and I look forward to the next time. We should get together a little earlier and maybe have a pint or two, just like old times. We wont overdo it, as we used to, but it would still be a nice break.

I am keeping well. Work is a bit of a bind but there again, isn't all work nowadays. Very stressy. Take care mate, see you soon I hope.

Cheers
Dave

As you can see, this letter is full of the elements that have been advised against in a business letter. This is precisely because personal letters are personal and you are often talking to people with whom you have built up a relationship over the years. You know and understand the person and the type of language that is acceptable, therefore the use of clichés, jargon and so on is perfectly acceptable.

In many ways, the personal letter is the opposite of the business letter in that, in the business letter, you are trying to portray a positive image, well constructed and to the point with the express aim of communicating your message in a formal way.

You would certainly never handwrite a business letter, or finish by saying 'cheers'.

In some cases, with a personal letter, you may wish to adopt a mix of formal and personal. If you were writing to your Uncle Tom, who you have not seen for twenty years, you would not be writing in a very chummy style and yet you would not be over-personal either. You would use some elements of intimacy connected with the family and family memories but you would also be looking to present a rather formal image as you do not know this person well enough to adopt a chummy approach.

The art and craft of writing personal letters very much depends on you as a person, the person you are communicating to and also what you are trying to say. If you are in correspondence with a friend or acquaintance who is interested in politics and you are discussing political events then you would probably need to be well versed in the language and grammar, as well as current affairs, to be able to express yourself effectively.

If you are discussing matters of the heart then you would need to be possessed of a language and style that allowed you to express yourself sensitively. In many cases, the advantage of knowing the English language, and the ability to express your self, bringing into play all the elements of language, such as grammar and punctuation, will prove to be a great asset. It is hoped that the brief introduction contained within this book will assist that process.

Now read the key points from Chapter 9 overleaf.

****

Key points from Chapter 9

- Personal letters have a different starting point to business letters.

- Although personal letters are less formal than business letters, there are still formal conventions to be followed.

- The personal letter will differ to the business letter in that the writer will normally put their name and address on the right hand side.

- The letter will finish with a variety of different endings depending who you are writing to.

Chapter 10

Editing and proofreading

Editing and proofreading letters is perhaps one of the most important elements in the production of effective letters, whether business or personal.

An effective editor/proof reader will need a range of skills, including a sound knowledge of the English language and of the intricacies of grammar. This book has, hopefully, allowed the reader to absorb the basic structure of the language.

You should always allow time for proof reading and understand that the task is part of the process of producing a letter.

Focussing on proof reading

Many environments are not ideal for proofreading so you should try to find a space where you can work comfortably without interruption. If your letter is complex or technical you may prefer to enlist some help to read the 'dead' copy (first draft) while you concentrate on producing the live (original) copy. Proof reading is about detail. However, we need to be aware of the broader impression of the piece of writing. You should proof read for:

- visual impression
- sense of the message
- accuracy of the detail.

Visual impression

What does the page look like? Is there too much detail on the page and is there enough white space? Is the page balanced between top and bottom and if there is a large gap at the bottom is this intended? Is the text justified? Is it aligned to the left only? Are headings too large or small and is the size of typeface appropriate?

Reading for sense

This aspect can test your knowledge of grammar and ability to write clearly.

Are the paragraph breaks in the right place and are sentences too long? Is there enough variety in the sentence structure? Are there errors of grammar and is the word order correct? Is the message of the letter clear?

Reading for detail

You should expect to find errors at the start of the text and near other errors. In addition, errors will appear in common words which are usually mixed up, such as:

- not/no
- there/the
- and/an

Errors will also appear when repeating from the end of a line to the beginning of the next line, in changes from standard type and in changes of page formation: margins, columns etc.

It is easy to rationalise these errors. Changes of type or page formation cause us to think about control instructions rather than the flow of typing. Some word processing software will not show the end of one line and the beginning of the next line simultaneously on the monitor.

You will be reassured by the relative ease with which you will find errors such as omitted letters, spaces, punctuation marks or substitutions of one letter for another. You will also be aware of the need to concentrate carefully when you proof read a letter properly You should ensure that you proof read a letter twice to ensure that you have not missed mistakes.

Check you are clear and concise

No single aspect of your writing will produce a clear, concise style: you will need to review a number of elements.

Sequence

- check that your letter achieves a progression of ideas
- see that you move from where you are at the start to where you want to be at the end.

Paragraphs

A paragraph that might suit a long report can look excessive when applied to another letter:

- make paragraphs in letters relatively short
- make the topic of each paragraph clear
- if you have divided a paragraph, see that the new paragraph has a clear headline and is not left dangling by a pronoun.

Sentences

- check your sentence length
- aim for an average of twenty words but vary your sentence length for interest.
- Remember that a series of short sentences can read like a menu.

Punctuation

- see that punctuation properly supports the structure of your writing. Be sure the reader will absorb the meaning in a single reading.
- If the punctuation is struggling to reveal your meaning rewrite the sentence

Active voice

- link subject and verb directly by presenting your case in the active voice.

Familiar words

- use familiar words that will be comfortable for the reader

Concrete words

-   use concrete words to paint a clear picture for the reader.
-   Make your specification explicit and complete

Cliches

-   avoid over- used business expressions
-   use your own words to set the right tone and help a flow of ideas.

Jargon

-   Use jargon to tune in to the reader
-   Avoid jargon that will sound out of tune.

Fulfil your aim

-   Ask yourself key questions:
-   who will read my letter?
-   What does my reader need to know?
-   What did I need to know?
-   Is the required action clear?
-   Will the reader know when to respond?

*

Proof reading and editing is an important skill and it is essential that letters are read and amended as necessary. Treat your first letter as a first draft that will need fine-tuning before you send it. If you are writing a particularly emotive letter, sometimes it is better to sleep on it for a night rather than send it immediately.

Now read the key points from chapter 10 overleaf.

****

Key points from Chapter 10

- Editing and proofreading is one of the most important elements when writing a letter, particularly a business letter.

- An effective proof-reader will need a range of skills, including a sound knowledge of the English language.

- Proof reading is about detail.

- In addition to detail you should be aware of the broader impression of a piece of writing, such as visual impression, sense of message and accuracy of detail.

Chapter 11

Writing Effective emails

The nature of business communication has, in particular changed due to COVID 19. There has been, without doubt an increase in email communication and communication by other media such as Zoom

In the previous chapters, we have covered business and personal letters. In this chapter we will cover business emails and also e mails that cover job applications and also marketing emails.

Business emails

In many cases now, whereas once upon a time a letter was necessary to confirm a deal or to agree on a business deal, now it is quite common to use an e mail. Because email is a rather different form of correspondence then it follows that there are slightly different rules to follow.

Although emails are often seen as less formal than printed business letters, in the business world you cannot afford to let your language appear to be informal. Email may be faster and more efficient, but your client or business partner will not easily forgive correspondence that is too casual.

Begin with a greeting

It's important to always open your email with a greeting, such as "Dear Peter,". Depending on the formality of your relationship, you may want to use their family name as opposed to their given name, i.e. "Dear Mrs. Davies,". If the relationship is more casual, you can simply say, "Hi Susan," If you're contacting a company, not an individual, you may write "To Whom It May Concern:" Thank the recipient If you are replying to a client's inquiry, you should begin with a line of thanks. For example, if someone has a question about your company, you can say, "Thank you for contacting (XXX) Company."

If someone has replied to one of your emails, be sure to say, "Thank you for your prompt reply." or "Thanks for getting back to me." If you can find any way to thank the reader, then do. It will put him or her at ease, and it will make you appear more courteous.

State your purpose

If, however, you are initiating the email communication, it may be impossible to include a line of thanks. Instead, begin by stating your purpose. For example, "I am writing to enquire about ..." or "I am writing in reference to ..." It's important to make your purpose clear early on in the email, and then move into the main text of your email.

Good Grammar!

Remember to pay careful attention to grammar, spelling and punctuation, and to avoid run-on sentences by keeping your sentences short and clear.

Closing remarks

Before you end your email, it's polite to thank your reader one more time as well as add some courteous closing remarks. You might start with "Thank you for your patience and cooperation." or "Thank you for your consideration." and then follow up with, "If you have any questions or concerns, don't hesitate to let me know." and "I look forward to hearing from you." End with a closing The last step is to include an appropriate closing with your name. "Best regards,"

"Sincerely," and "Thank you," are all professional. It's a good idea to avoid closings such as "Best wishes," or "Cheers," as these are best used in casual, personal emails. Finally, before you hit the send button, review and spell check your email one more time to make sure it's truly perfect!

The following are some tips to help you when you are writing business letters through email.

- A heading is not necessary in an email (your return address, their address, and the date).
- Use a descriptive subject line.
- Avoid using an inappropriate or silly email address; register a professional sounding address if you don't have one.
- Use simple formatting, keep everything flush with the left margin; avoid special formatting and tabs.
- Keep your letter formal, just because it's an email instead of a hard copy is no excuse for informality (don't forget to use spell check and proper grammar).
- Try to keep your letter less than 80 characters wide, some email readers will create line breaks on anything longer and ruin the formatting.

- If possible, avoid attachments unless the recipient has requested or is expecting an attachment. If it is a text document, simply cut and paste the text below your letter and strip out any special formatting.
- If the person's name is unknown, address the person's title e.g. Dear Director of Human Resources.

Job application emails

As with business emails, it is now common to email companies with CV's, job applications and cover letters. Your covering email is quite important as this is quite often the first thing that a prospective employer might see. First impressions can be lasting impressions!

Subject line

After you have checked that you have the right email address, you need to make sure that you put the right information in the subject line. This immediately shows the respondent what the email is about and ensures that it does not get overlooked or counted as spam.

*

Addressing the email

In the same way as a covering letter, a covering email should be addressed to the right person as outline don the job specification. Be sure to address the recipient in the correct manner, either as 'Mr' or 'Mrs' or 'Ms' (if you are not sure of status). If the job specification simply states 'S. Wilson' then just address sit S Wilson as guessing can be quite insulting if you get it wrong.

If you are applying for a job that requires an initial covering letter then it is a good idea to keep your email short and to the point. One paragraph is enough which should act as an introduction to you as a person, what you can bring to the company in question and why you are applying for the position.

Attachments

If you need to attach your CV and covering letter to your email, there are a few things that you need to be wary about. Firstly, make sure that your documents are named correctly.- simply calling your CV 'CV' isn't very descriptive, especially when your potential employer is likely to be drowning in them. make sure you include your name when naming your documents and be sure to actually attach them to your email before sending. Its surprising how many people forget!

When signing off your email, you should try to end with something positive and polite like; "Thank you for taking the time to review my application. I look forward to hearing from you". This will show that you are enthusiastic and polite, two attributes that all employers want to see.

Also be sure to sign off with "Kind Regards" or "Yours Sincerely" rather than something chatty or informal.

Taking time over your email should help you in your quest for a job. First impressions, lasting impressions!

Email marketing

According to some estimates, more than 144 billion emails are sent every day—and, sometimes, it seems like every one of them lands in your inbox. We all know what it's like to be bombarded with email messages—all competing for a share of our attention during a busy day.

There are certain rules to adopt when using emails for the purpose of marketing. As we all know, marketing emails can seem annoying and irrelevant. We delete them more often than not. There is also the problem of spam and what it might do to your computer. Below are a few tips to help you construct an effective marketing e mail which might get read.

If it's your job to come up with a subject line that is compelling enough to cut through all that clutter, it's a good idea to apply your experience as an email recipient to help you craft the perfect subject line. What gets your attention? How do you decide which emails to trash unopened and which to read? Scores of scientific studies can tell you which words appear with the most frequency in successful email campaigns. And that is useful information.

But in creating a compelling subject line, sometimes a simple strategy works best.

Keep it brief

When prospects are scanning their inboxes, a short, snappy subject is more likely to catch their eye than a lengthier line. If possible, it's best to keep the subject line short enough to appear as one line on a smaller device screen, such as a smartphone or tablet.

Don't waste valuable space

A subject line doesn't provide much space, so make every word count. Don't waste space with words (such as "hello") that don't add much value to your message. When crafting your subject line, evaluate each word and make sure it adds value—from the standpoint of providing information or encouraging readers to open the email.

Be specific

When readers are scanning new messages in their inbox, they're generally in a hurry to respond to urgent messages or tackle the next task in their busy day. In such a state of mind, they won't have much patience for mystery. Cut to the chase by using the subject line to tell them what the message is about.

Make it searchable

There's a good chance your reader won't have time to focus on your message when they first see it, so it's wise to give them an easy way to return to the message when they have more time. If you make the subject line searchable so readers can easily find it later, there's a better chance that they'll revisit your email, even if they don't have time at first.

Include a call to action

Make sure your subject line tells the reader what he or she can do to benefit from the message—whether that's to visit a site, make a call, or just read the message. A brief line that summarizes the value can be highly effective, so think about what's in it for the reader and try to convey that in the subject line.

Don't create anxiety

Although you want your readers to take action, it's important to balance a call to action with a signal that you respect their time. Subject lines that include phrases such as "immediate response required" can come across as arrogant. Adding "FYI" or "no need to reply" can take the pressure off while still signalling that the message contains valuable information.

Include your company name

Readers will be more likely to open an email if they know who it's from and if they perceive value from the sending organization. Including a company name is especially important if you already have a positive relationship with the reader.

Email is one of the major ways how we communicate in business. The issue isn't email itself, but inbox overload and finding a way to separate the mundane and annoying from the truly important. There are proven ways to tame overflowing inboxes, and every professional needs a sound strategy. Your challenge as an email marketer is to ensure that your message makes the cut.

****

12

Hints on Texting Business Colleagues and Clients

Texting and other forms of electronic communications are on the rise, both personal texts and in the workplace. The Pandemic has resulted in a rise in texts as well as emails. So, in the workplace, when is it appropriate to text a colleague?

Texting a colleague generally depends on how casual your relationship is, what you're texting the person about and what this person's seniority level is. Texting is fairly personal, indeed, our phones have become an extension of our personalities to some degree, and texting a form of direct messaging. The problem with texting, however, is that it can lose context.

When texting a colleague, you should consider the following rules of etiquette:

1. Texting your manager

Texting your manager has become increasingly necessary, especially when an issue is urgent or needs to be resolved quickly. When you do text, you should be communicating simple messages such as meeting times and places. Or text when the message requires an immediate response or requests a coffee meeting. Never text bad news about a contract, an important decisions or a message that includes abbreviations. Everything should be kept professional. Of course, you should always respond to any inquiries your manager texts to you.

If the manager is younger and/or running a small business, texting language may be more colloquial. If you're not sure, refer to your corporate communications policy.

2. Texting team members

In general, you should be cautious when texting team members. These messages may depend on age, gender, personal relationship and even hours. Everything you write might be relayed to other team members and to managers. Screenshots can be taken of everything you write and passed on, then taken out of context.

When in doubt, be professional!

Take into consideration your recipients' relationship status and emotional state, and remember that texts lose context. These messages can also be misconstrued by your significant others and cause problems at home, even if they're an inside joke.

Try not to text team members after working hours unless you have a personal relationship with them outside of work. If you feel like you want to text them about work after 5 pm, use email.

Texting your prospective client

This is a hotly debated topic in the sales community in particular. Texting your prospective client is dependent on the type of rapport you have, whether this individual has given permission and where in the sales process you are. Never cold-call through text messaging. Many people believe that text messaging is still a personal communication that requires urgent attention, and that texting people you're soliciting business from when you don't know them is considered gauche.

If however you have a good rapport with your prospect, texting during business hours can be appropriate if it's about finding a meeting place, notifying this person that you are running late to a meeting, following up to a question or providing something of value. Being pushy about closing a deal using a text is not recommended.

Texting networking colleagues

For the most part, networking colleagues whom you're exchanging business information with can be fair game. Starting with email is traditional, typically. But people who are networking may be excited about helping each another with business development. So this relationship often escalates to texting fairly quickly. Once again, your texting relationship depends on gender and age. Younger members of the same sex are more likely to find it appropriate.

How to encourage less texting

Is texting making you or your colleagues angry? Want to encourage fewer texts to your phone after hours? Here are some tips to decrease texts and keep your mobile phone free of business during your personal time:

• Stop including your mobile phone on your business cards

- Convey your own communication policy in your email signature.
- Exclude your mobile phone and add a line specifically requesting, *Please send all correspondence via email.*
- Ask those contacting you to communicate only during business hours, and if they need to send you work, to send it only through email. Entrepreneurs and freelancers may forget that others aren't working at their odd hours.
- For major offenders, start using the Do Not Disturb feature on your cell phone during the weekends and evenings.
- Walk into any boardroom two minutes before a meeting and you'll find the same scenario: a table full of executives checking their phones with their heads bowed in the "smartphone prayer."

****

Summary

Text messaging is the fastest way to communicate in business. Quicker than email and more convenient than a phone call, it's become commonplace. But it's not always the best choice.

Choose to text messages for simple notifications or reminders like "I'm running five minutes late," or "Remember to bring the report." As a general rule, consider texting only appropriate for a maximum of two messages -- one message and one reply. Below are five rules to avoid a text message business blunder.

1. Keep it positive.

Like email, the tone of a text message can be misinterpreted by the recipient. Quick messages can make you come off as flippant or harsh. Instead of staccato phrases, write complete sentences. Add polite touches like "please" and "thank you." Re-read every message before pressing send to double-check your tone

2. Avoid serious topics.

You wouldn't break up with your girlfriend over a text message -- to be clear, you should not -- and the same goes for business. Never give negative feedback or fire someone via a text message. Any serious conversation should take place face-to-face. It allows for subtle interaction through facial expressions and will ensure clear communication.

3. Don't abbreviate every other word.

Abbreviations are common in casual texts, but you should be careful how often you use them. Common abbreviations like "LOL" (laugh out loud) and "np" (no problem) are safe choices. However, if you're communicating with a new customer or acquaintance, take 30 extra seconds and type out each word.

Avoid informal shortcuts like "u" (you) and less common abbreviations like "SMH" (shaking my head) or "MFW" (my face when). Don't leave your clients and colleagues confused; your texts should convey messages quickly and clearly.

4. Don't text a last-minute cancellation.

There are a thousand reasons someone may miss a text message. Don't depend on a quick note to cancel a meeting or change a lunch venue. For an important or time-sensitive message, pick up the phone.

5. Double-check the autocorrect.

Smart phones can occasionally be a little too smart. Autocorrect and voice-to-text features have a sneaky way of changing your intended message into something entirely different and often embarrassing. When using voice-to-text, ensure you're in a quiet location. It picks up on background noise and may type a nearby conversation instead of what you're saying.

****

Glossary of terms

Acronym. A word formed from the initial letters of other words.

Adjective. A word that describes a noun.

Adverb. A word that qualifies a verb, an adjective or other adverb.

Clause, dependent. A main group of words containing a verb that depends on the main clause. They cannot stand alone.

Conjunction. A word that links two main clauses together.

Gerund. A present participle used as a noun.

Inverted commas. Speech marks put around speech and quotations.

Jargon. Words or expressions used by a certain group of people.

Justify. Adjust margins so that they are level.

Metaphor. An implied comparison of two things.

Noun, abstract. A word that denotes a quality or state.

Noun, collective. A singular word which refers to a group of people or things.

Noun, common. The name of a thing.

Noun, proper. The name of a person or place. It always begins with a capital letter.

Object. A noun or pronoun that follows the verb and is related to the subject.

Paragraph. A group of sentences dealing with the same topic.

Personify. Giving a humane object human characteristics.

Phrase. A group of words not necessarily containing a verb or making sense on its own.

Preposition. A word that governs a noun or pronoun.

Pronoun, interrogative. A pronoun that is used at the start of a question.

Pronoun, personal. A word that takes the place of a noun.

Pronoun, relative. This has a similar role to a conjunction. It joins clauses together but is closely linked to a noun.

Simile. A comparison of two things using 'like' or 'as'.

Subject. The noun or pronoun on which the rest of the clause depends.

Synonym. A word that can be used to replace another.

Tautology. A statement that is repeated in a different way in the same sentence.

Thesaurus. A book which will give a collection of synonyms.

Index

****

www.straightforwardco.co.uk

All titles, listed below, in the Straightforward Guides Series can be purchased online, using credit card or other forms of payment by going to www.straightfowardco.co.uk A discount of 25% per title is offered with online purchases.

Law

A Straightforward Guide to:

Consumer Rights

Bankruptcy Insolvency and the Law

Employment Law

Private Tenants Rights

Family law

Small Claims in the County Court

Contract law

Intellectual Property and the law

Divorce and the law

Leaseholders Rights

The Process of Conveyancing

Knowing Your Rights and Using the Courts

Producing Your own Will

Housing Rights

The Bailiff the law and You

Probate and The Law

Company law

What to Expect When You Go to Court

Give me Your Money-Guide to Effective Debt Collection

Caring for a Disabled Child

General titles

Letting Property for Profit

Buying, Selling and Renting property

Buying a Home in England and France

Bookkeeping and Accounts for Small Business

Creative Writing

Freelance Writing

Writing Your own Life Story

Writing performance Poetry

Writing Romantic Fiction

Speech Writing

Creating a Successful Commercial Website

The Straightforward Business Plan

The Straightforward C.V.

Successful Public Speaking

Handling Bereavement

Individual and Personal Finance

Understanding Mental Illness

The Two Minute Message

Crime Reference

The Crime Writers Handbook

Being a Detective

A Comprehensive Guide to Arrest and Detention

A Comprehensive Guide to Burglary and Robbery

A Comprehensive Guide to Drink and Disorder

Go to: www.straightforwardco.co.uk